LEARN ABOUT

THE SEA

R O B I N   K E R R O D

LORENZ BOOKS
LONDON • NEW YORK • SYDNEY • BATH

This edition published in the UK in 1997 by Lorenz Books

Lorenz Books is an imprint of
Anness Publishing Limited
Hermes House
88–89 Blackfriars Road
London SE1 8HA

This edition is distributed in Canada by Raincoast Books,
8680 Cambie Street, Vancouver, British Columbia, V6P 6MP

Publisher: Joanna Lorenz
Managing Editor, Children's Books: Sue Grabham
Project Editor: Sophie Warne
Editors: Jenny Fry and Ros Carreck
Consultant: Bryan Bett
Photographer: John Freeman
Stylists: Marion Elliot and Melanie Williams
Designer: Caroline Grimshaw
Picture Researcher: Liz Eddison
Illustrators: Stephen Sweet and John Whetton

Printed and bound in China
1 3 5 7 9 10 8 6 4 2

The Publishers would like to thank the following children,
and their parents, for modelling in this book –
Emily Askew, Sarah Barnes, Maria Bloodworth, Lawrence De Freitas,
Alistair Fulton, Anton Golbourne, Kira Hartop, Alex Lindblom Smith,
Sophie Lindblom Smith, Kerry Jane Morgan.

THE SEA

CONTENTS

4 • The restless sea

6 • At the seaside

8 • Sea world

10 • Birth of the seas

12 • Drifting continents

14 • Underwater landscape

16 • The salty sea

18 • Salty waters

20 • Waves and currents

22 • Making waves

24 • The tides

26 • Ocean edge

28 • The changing coastline

30 • Islands

32 • Life in the oceans

34 • Shore life

36 • On the shore

38 • Sea birds

40 • Watching the birds

42 • Life in the open sea

44 • Sea mammals

46 • Life on a coral reef

48 • Ships

50 • Floating and hovering

52 • Submarines

54 • Up periscope

56 • Diving

58 • Dive, dive, dive

60 • The sea's resources

62 • Saving the seas

64 • Index

THE RESTLESS SEA

I f you were an alien visiting our planet from Space, you would see the Earth as a blue planet with scattered brown patches. The vast areas coloured blue are water, and the brown patches are land. Over 70 percent of the Earth's surface is covered with water, which forms a huge world sea, or ocean. If you tasted the seawater, you would find that it was very salty, unlike the freshwater in rivers and lakes.

The sea has many fascinating rhythms and ever-changing moods as the waves pound the shore and the tides flow in and out. It teems with a variety of life, from microscopic single-celled creatures to monster whales weighing up to 150 tonnes. You do not have to be an alien to discover the secrets of the sea. You can start finding out for yourself when you visit the seaside, and find how fascinating the sea can be.

Many holidaymakers visit the seaside in the summer months, where they can sunbathe, swim or sail boats.

In stormy weather, huge waves crash against the rocks, reminding us how powerful and dangerous the sea is. The constant battering of the waves will, in time, break up the toughest rocks into tiny pieces. The daily pounding of the waves also cuts into cliffs, making caves and arches. Collapsed arches leave pillars of rock called stacks.

Heavyweights

A humpback whale and her calf cruise in their watery habitat. Blue whales are the largest creatures of the sea, weighing up to 150 tonnes. They spend most of their time underwater, but as mammals they do have to surface in order to breathe.

On a coral reef in Indonesia, a grouper is eating a long-nosed butterfly fish. These two kinds of fish are common on coral reefs around the world.

Sail and steam

In 1838, the *Great Western* was the first steamship to provide a regular service across the Atlantic Ocean. It was built by the British engineer Isambard Kingdom Brunel and sailed between Bristol, in south-west England, and New York, on the east coast of the USA. It was built of wood and powered by paddle wheels, but it had sails in case the engine failed.

AT THE SEASIDE

We all like going to the seaside on a summer's day to swim, to explore the beach or to play games on the sand. The seashore is also a fascinating place to investigate. Something interesting is always happening as the waves crash down and the tide rolls in and out twice a day. There is usually plenty of wildlife to be found – in the sea, in the air, on the beach, hidden away under the sand or in rock pools. One way to learn about the plants and animals that live there is to check out a section of the shore. The first project will show you how to do it. Then you can make an underwater viewer. It will help you to spot water creatures more easily because it cuts out the reflections from the surface, which usually spoil your view. When you visit the seaside, remember to take along your field guides to identify the plants and animals that you see.

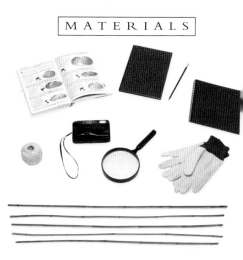

You will need: gloves, roll of string, bamboo canes, magnifying glass, camera, field guides, notebook and pencil.

Investigating the shore

1 At low tide, stretch the string from the edge of the sea to the top of the beach. Use canes to hold up the string. Walk the length of the string, noting down what you see.

2 At the top of the beach you will find one or two species of land plants that are able to live in the salty environment. Use a magnifying glass to investigate the plants.

3 A notable place on the shore is the high water mark, where seaweed, dead fish and driftwood are deposited by the high tide. Seaweed flies and sandhoppers live there.

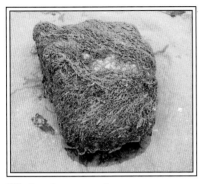

4 On the upper shore, you may find this green seaweed clinging to exposed rocks. Use your camera and notebook to keep records.

5 Farther down, on the middle shore, wide banks of brown seaweed, called wrack, can often be found. So can clusters of barnacles.

6 You can find flat seaweed, called kelp, on the lower shore. The coming tide has carried it from the lowest part of the shore.

MATERIALS

You will need: pencil, scissors, self-adhesive plastic film, large diameter plastic pipe or tube, strong elastic band.

WARNING

Do not go near the sea by yourself, and take care when walking on wet, slippery rocks. Watch out for the tide coming in, and beware of fishing hooks, broken glass or rubbish on the shore. Always wear gloves while collecting shells and plants from the seashore.

Make an underwater viewer

1 Cut a circle out of the plastic film about 2–3 cm larger all round than the diameter of the pipe. Peel off the back to expose the sticky surface.

2 Stick the film over the bottom of the pipe, pressing it firmly. Fit the elastic band tightly round it, to make sure of a watertight fit.

3 Push the end of your viewer into the water and look down the pipe. You should be able to see creatures under the water more clearly.

SEA WORLD

This is a tiny coral island in the Pacific Ocean. Coral islands are surrounded by reefs, which are built by tiny sea creatures called polyps. The polyps deposit hard limey cups around their bodies, which other polyps build on.

Ice-cold
The Arctic is the smallest ocean in the world. It is almost surrounded by the great land masses of Europe, Asia, North America and Greenland.

Seawater covers almost 370 million square kilometres, or about 70 percent, of the Earth's surface. We divide this vast area into seven oceans, although it is really just one continuous body of water. There are five main oceans – the Pacific, Atlantic, Indian, Arctic and the Antarctic, which is also called the Southern Ocean. The largest oceans, the Pacific and Atlantic, can be divided into northern and southern parts by the Equator, which gives us seven oceans in all. Sailors used to refer to them as the Seven Seas. Although seas and oceans are thought to mean the same thing, a sea really refers to a smaller body of water within the larger oceans, often partly enclosed by land. The North Sea between the British Isles and continental Europe is an example.

When you look at a map or globe of the world, you can see that the sea covers most of the surface. The largest expanses of sea form the Pacific, Atlantic and Indian Oceans.

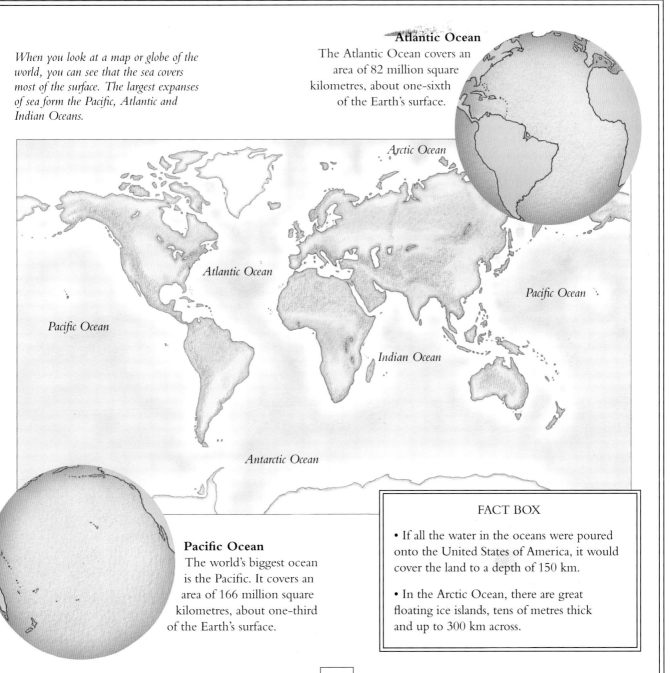

Atlantic Ocean

The Atlantic Ocean covers an area of 82 million square kilometres, about one-sixth of the Earth's surface.

Arctic Ocean

Atlantic Ocean

Pacific Ocean

Pacific Ocean

Indian Ocean

Antarctic Ocean

Pacific Ocean

The world's biggest ocean is the Pacific. It covers an area of 166 million square kilometres, about one-third of the Earth's surface.

FACT BOX

• If all the water in the oceans were poured onto the United States of America, it would cover the land to a depth of 150 km.

• In the Arctic Ocean, there are great floating ice islands, tens of metres thick and up to 300 km across.

BIRTH OF THE SEAS

When the Earth was born, some 4,500 million years ago, there were no oceans. The Earth was far too hot, and so water only existed as vapour. When the Earth began to cool down, the water vapour condensed into storm clouds, and rain began to fall. Eventually water began to form pools on the surface, and nearly 1,000 million years later the oceans were born. The early oceans and continents were not in the same places as they are today. This is because the Earth's crust is divided into plates that cover the Earth like the six-sided shapes on a football. In some places beneath the oceans, the plates are moving apart and the ocean floor is widening. In others, the plates are moving together. When two plates meet, one slides beneath the other, dragging the seabed down into the depths of an ocean trench where it is destroyed in the molten rock.

The world as it looks today. It will not always look like this because the continents are still on the move.

200 million years ago

100 million years ago

50 million years ago

Drifting continents
About 200 million years ago, all of today's continents were combined in the great land mass, Pangaea. There was also one great world sea, known as Panthalassa. Then Pangaea began to break up as the plates of the Earth's crust started to move. The North Atlantic Ocean opened up first and slowly widened. About 100 million years ago, the South Atlantic began to grow as South America split from Africa. South America only joined up with North America about 5 million years ago. About 50 million years ago these two continents were still separate land masses.

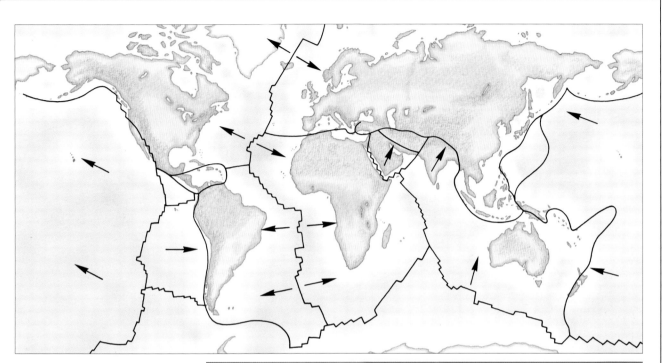

The moving plates

This map of the world shows that the Earth's crust is split into 13 huge pieces, called plates. These plates are drifting together or moving apart very slowly. The arrows show the direction in which the plates are moving.

A view of the northern end of the Red Sea, which divides Africa (left) from Arabia. A boundary between two plates runs through the middle of the Red Sea. One plate is carrying Arabia ever eastwards.

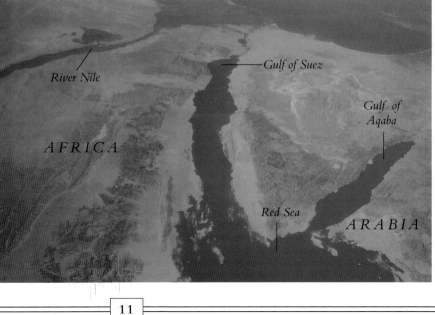

River Nile

Gulf of Suez

Gulf of Aqaba

AFRICA

Red Sea

ARABIA

DRIFTING CONTINENTS

The rocky plates that form the Earth's crust and carry the continents and sea floor are always on the move. In places, plates slide smoothly past one another. However, sometimes they jam and then suddenly jerk free, which creates earthquakes. Elsewhere, plates are colliding, and the pressure causes the surface to wrinkle and form fold mountains. The great mountain range of the Andes in South America was formed, and is still changing, because a plate under the Pacific Ocean is colliding with the South American plate. In the middle of the Atlantic Ocean different kinds of plate movements are taking place. The plate carrying North America is moving apart from the plate carrying Europe. It is causing the Atlantic Ocean to get wider year by year.

Colliding plates
Make a sandwich of layers of modelling clay. Push it from each end to see how colliding plates create fold mountains *(left)*.

A continental jigsaw

You will need: sheets of tracing paper, pencil, atlas, sticky tape, sheets of coloured card, scissors.

1 Find the continents of North and South America, Europe and Africa in an atlas. Trace the outlines of the shape of these continents on to tracing paper.

2 Stick the tracing paper onto different coloured sheets of card. Then carefully cut around the outlines of the continents you have drawn from the atlas.

3 Move the eastern (right-hand) coasts of North and South America up to the western (left-hand) coasts of Europe and Africa to see how well they fit together.

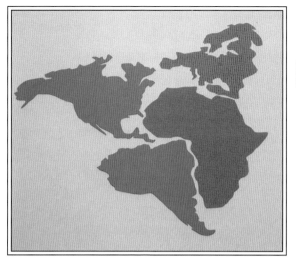

4 You will find that the coastlines of the Americas, Europe and Africa fit together quite well. Scientists believe that these continents were once joined together in this way.

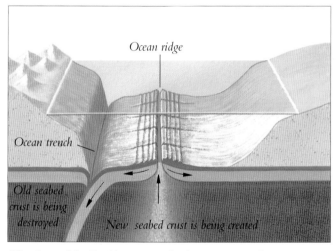

Ocean ridge

Ocean trench

Old seabed crust is being destroyed

New seabed crust is being created

The plates of the Earth's crust are slowly moving over the hot, soft rock that lies beneath it. In some areas, such as the Mid-Atlantic Ridge, the plates are moving apart. Molten rock rises to plug the gap, creating new seabed rocks. In other parts, one plate slides beneath another to create ocean trenches, which are the deepest places on Earth. This process, which is called subduction, can create volcanoes or earthquakes.

Plates on the move

The continents of the Americas, Europe and Africa sit on plates that are moving in opposite directions. Use the continent cards you have made to see how they drift apart. Fold a large sheet of paper in half and attach paperclips along the fold. Drape it over two boxes. Stick the Americas on one sheet and Europe and Africa on the other. Push upwards on the fold and see the continents move apart.

UNDERWATER LANDSCAPE

You might think that the sea floor is flat and featureless, but you would be wrong. Deep down on the seabed there are vast flat plains, great ranges of mountains and deep valleys, called trenches or deeps. The deepest valleys and tallest mountains on Earth are found under the sea. There are also great fractures, or gashes, and many volcanoes. At the edges of the continents the oceans form a shallow region called the continental shelf. At the outer edge of the shelf, the seabed drops gently away down to the ocean floor.

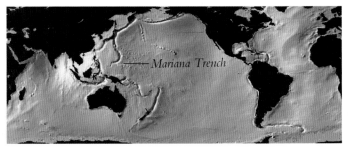

Seeing the seabed
The world's deepest waters are in the Mariana Trench at Challenger Deep. Satellites help us to plot these great trenches on the ocean floor.

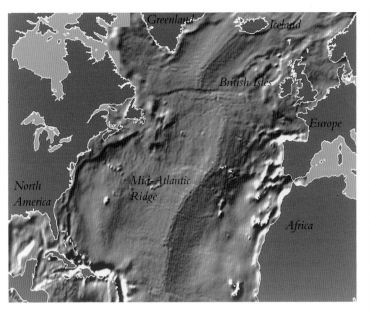

New seabed is being created along the crest of the Mid-Atlantic Ridge. It then moves away to each side as new rock wells up from below.

FACT BOX
• Under the oceans, the Earth's crust is, on average, about 10 km thick. This is about a quarter as thick as the continental crust.

• The Mid-Atlantic Ridge is part of a 50,000 km long mountain range.

• In places close to mid-ocean ridges, there are vents, or holes, in the sea floor. Liquids and gases containing minerals stream out of these vents from the hot rocks beneath. They are called smokers because of the smoke-like effect that is produced when the hot minerals mix with the cold seawater.

• Parts of the Pacific ocean floor are scattered with metal-rich chunks, called manganese nodules.

Submarine wonders

The amazing landscape of the sea floor of the Atlantic Ocean. The most dominant feature is the snaking S-shaped Mid-Atlantic Ridge. This is where new sea floor is being created from beneath and marks the boundary between crustal plates moving eastwards and westwards. Other features of the sea floor include vast flat plain regions, isolated seamounts and numerous mountains that poke out of the water as islands.

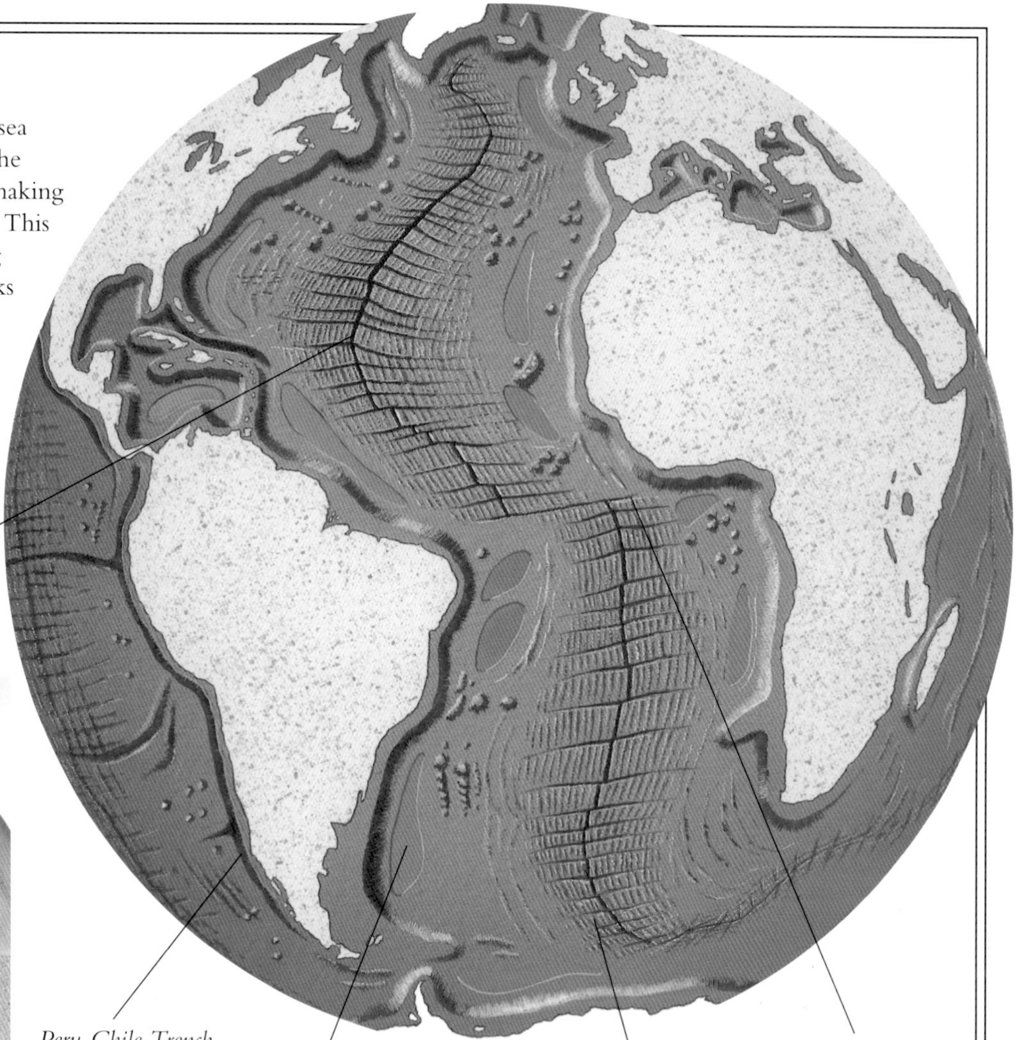

Mid-Atlantic Ridge (North)

Mount Everest

Challenger Deep

Peru-Chile Trench

Argentine Abyssal Plain

Mid-Atlantic Ridge (South)

Romanche Fracture Zone

Beating Everest

Mount Everest is the world's highest mountain on land, soaring to 8,848 m above sea level. The deepest point in the sea is the Challenger Deep, in the Pacific Ocean, which descends to 11,034 m.

THE SALTY SEA

Seawater is very salty and not fit for drinking. This is because it contains about 3.5 percent of dissolved minerals, or salts (although the salinity, or saltiness, of the water varies from place to place). The main salt is sodium chloride, or common salt. There are also large amounts of magnesium, potassium and calcium salts. Rivers are the main source of these salts. As they flow over the rocks on land, they slowly dissolve the rocks' minerals and carry them into the sea. Some lakes are salty for the same reason – the largest are often called 'seas'.

The saltiness of seawater stays about the same because the amount of water in the sea remains more or less constant. This happens because of the water cycle.

These pie charts show the amount of dissolved salts in seawater and the main substances in the salts.

Swimmers float easily in the waters of the Dead Sea because there is so much salt dissolved in the water.

This beautiful mineral is called a desert rose after its rose-like shape. It is a crystalline form of gypsum, a common mineral found dissolved in seawater.

Salty crust
A thick salt crust covers this salt lake in the Tirari Desert in South Australia. The salt remained when the water evaporated in the Sun's heat.

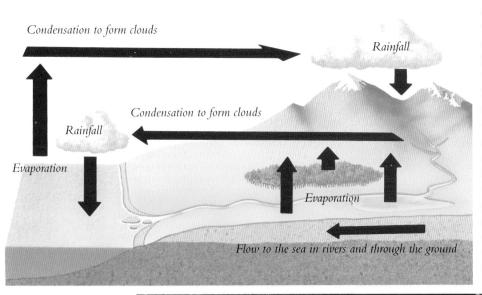

Condensation to form clouds

Rainfall

Condensation to form clouds

Rainfall

Evaporation

Evaporation

Flow to the sea in rivers and through the ground

Circulating water

The amount of water in the sea remains the same because of the water cycle. The cycle begins when the Sun evaporates water from the sea into the air as vapour. This rises and cools. As it does so, it condenses, or turns back to water, in the form of tiny droplets. The droplets gather together as clouds and fall back to the Earth as rain or snow. This water will eventually make its way back to the seas via rivers.

Underwater oxygen

There are fish that live in freshwater and fish that live in the sea. Very few fish can live in both freshwater and seawater. Like freshwater, seawater dissolves oxygen from the air. Fish take in the oxygen through their gills. Water enters the fish's mouth and passes over its gills, which take oxygen out of the seawater in the same way that our lungs take oxygen out of the air. The water then goes out through the gill slits.

SALTY WATERS

You will need: measuring jug, large glass container, weighing scales, salt, spoon.

On our planet there are over one million million million tonnes of seawater. In this first project you can make some more! It will not be exactly like real seawater, but it will be very close to it. This is because the ordinary table salt you will use is the same chemical compound as the salt found in the greatest quantity in seawater.

In the second project, you can find out how to make a hydrometer to measure the density of water. The word hydrometer means water measurer. Seawater is denser than freshwater because of the amount of salt dissolved in it. The higher the density of the water, the 'thicker' it becomes, and the more easily it supports an object floating in it. If you float your hydrometer in a container, you will find that it will sink lower into your tap water than it will in your 'seawater'.

Making seawater

1 Carefully fill the measuring jug with water up to the litre mark. Then pour the water into the large glass container and put it to one side until it is needed.

2 Using the weighing scales, measure out 35 g of ordinary table salt. Then add the salt little by little to the water in the glass container to make seawater.

3 Stir the water thoroughly until all the salt dissolves. Now scoop up some of the water in the spoon and take a sip. This is more or less what seawater tastes like.

You will need: scissors, drinking straw, modelling clay, glass container, pencil.

Making a hydrometer

1 Cut the straw in half. Roll some modelling clay up into a small ball. Push this onto one end of the straw. This is all you need to do to make a basic hydrometer.

2 Fill the container with tap water and place your hydrometer in it. Adjust the amount of modelling clay so that it just floats. Mark the water line on the straw.

3 Now place your hydrometer in the seawater you made in the first project. Check the water line on your straw. You will find that it is lower than it was before because seawater is denser than tap water.

Plimsoll lines
Plimsoll lines are a series of lines on the side of a ship showing how low the ship can safely sink when loaded in different water conditions. The top marking is TF, standing for Tropical Freshwater. It is at the top because the ship sinks lower in warm freshwater because of its lower density.

WAVES AND CURRENTS

The sea is never still. Waves are moving over its surface all the time. They are set in motion mainly by the wind. The stronger the winds, the higher the waves are. Waves can travel thousands of kilometres across the oceans. In the open sea they ripple across the surface as they travel, but the water itself does not move forwards with them. As the waves near the shore, water at the bottom of the wave drags on the seabed and the crests, or high points of the waves, crash onto the shore. Huge tidal waves, or tsunamis, are triggered off by earthquakes on the seabed.

In places, the water in the oceans moves in huge streams called currents. They can be hot or cold and have a marked effect on the climate. Winds cause most surface currents, but deep-water currents are caused by differences in temperature and density.

A surfer successfully rides an enormous breaker, or breaking wave.

Battering seas
A house collapsing into the sea on the east coast of England. When this house was built, it was some distance from the sea. Since then, however, constant battering by the waves has washed the cliffs away.

Currents from Space
Satellites can spot warm and cold currents in the oceans. This image shows the warm Gulf Stream current (pinkish beige) flowing north past Florida.

El Niño's effects

This damaging bush fire in Australia has been caused by the effects of the El Niño current on the weather. The El Niño is a sea current that moves across the Pacific Ocean. Every few years the winds weaken over the Pacific and the El Niño current surges in the opposite direction to its usual course. This has a dramatic impact on the weather conditions, such as severe drought or flooding, over vast areas.

World currents

This diagram shows the main warm and cold currents that circulate round the world. The direction of the currents is affected by the shape of the ocean and the spinning of the Earth. Notice how they circle clockwise in the oceans north of the Equator and anti-clockwise in those south of it. These currents move large bands of water through the oceans and also affect the climate of the land they pass by.

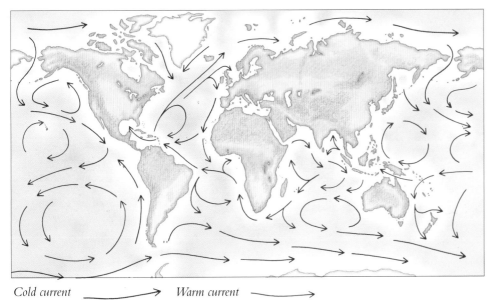

Cold current ⟶   *Warm current* ⟶

MAKING WAVES

Here, we take a closer look at waves and currents and investigate how they are produced. We see how the wind can cause both waves and currents in the water. Some of the purest water waves can also be seen when raindrops fall into a pond. Waves spread out in a series of perfect circles from the point where the raindrop enters the water. If you look carefully, you will see that the water itself does not move forward, just the wave, because waves travel across the surface of liquids. The water itself only moves up and down as the wave passes through it. You can confirm this in your experiment with the floats. See how they bob up and down but do not move forwards. Your experiment with a rope will show you what happens. The rope does not move forward as the waves ripple along it.

Wind and waves
Fill a tank with water and blow across the surface. The surface starts rippling, forming tiny waves. This is what happens to the sea when the wind blows.

Ever-increasing circles
When you drop a ball of modelling clay into the water, it sets up waves. The waves travel out in circles from the point where the ball entered the water.

Raindrop ripples
Raindrops make circular ripples when they fall on the water. The ripples grow larger, but the water itself does not move outwards.

Bobbing up and down

Place some small floats in a tank of water. Make waves at one end by hitting the water. Notice how the floats bob up and down but do not move forwards as the waves travel across the surface of the water.

A wavy rope

Ask a friend to hold one end of a rope while you hold the other. Let the rope sag. Now quickly flick your end up and down. The wave moves forwards along the rope. The rope itself only moves up and down.

Wind, waves and currents

Sprinkle coloured powder paint on the water in your tank. Blow gently over the surface and see the powder move. The air moving over the surface has set up currents in the water. This is also what happens at sea.

Wave approaches float

Float maintains position

Wave travels, float does not

Wave motion

These diagrams show how waves travel across the water surface, while objects floating in it hardly move at all.

THE TIDES

In most parts of the world, the seawater gradually rises then falls twice a day. These movements are called the tides. When the water is rising, we say the tide is flowing. When it is falling, we say the tide is ebbing. This movement of the ocean waters is caused by the gravitational pull of the Sun and the Moon, and by the Earth spinning. As the Moon circles round the Earth, it pulls at the ocean water directly beneath it, causing it to rise. A similar rise in sea level occurs on the opposite side of the Earth as the water bulges out as a result of the Earth spinning. At these places we witness a high tide. Some six hours later the Moon has passed on, in effect dragging the water with it. The sea falls to its lowest point, and we experience a low tide. The amount the tide rises and falls depends on how the Sun and the Moon are aligned with the Earth. The tide comes in further and goes out further on a spring tide. The tidal range is not nearly as great on a neap tide.

Magic Moon
Even though the Moon is quite a small body, it still has enough gravity to pull water in the Earth's oceans towards it.

Highs and lows

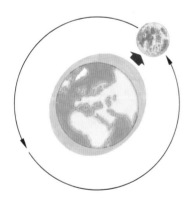

Tides rise as the Moon circles the spinning Earth. The gravity of the Moon tugs at the oceans, pulling the water round with it.

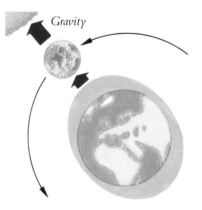

Gravity

Once a fortnight, the Sun and the Moon line up with the Earth. Their combined pull creates a spring tide.

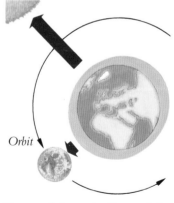

Orbit

One week later, the Sun and the Moon are at right angles to each other. Pulling in different directions, they create a neap tide.

High tide

It is high tide and these sailing boats are floating in the water. The sea has risen to its highest point on the shore.

Low tide

It is low tide. About six hours ago these sailing boats were floating in the water. Now the tide has gone right out, leaving them high and dry.

Beating the flood

The Thames tidal barrier on the outskirts of London, England, is designed to protect parts of inner London from flooding. This could happen if exceptionally high tides, driven on by gale force winds, swept up the River Thames from its estuary. The barrier stretches 520 m across the Thames and consists of 10 movable steel gates that are kept under the river bed. The gates are raised to form the barrier when danger threatens.

OCEAN EDGE

The mouth of the River Torridge in south-west England. Notice how the river has changed its course as a result of dropping its load of mud and pebbles.

The sea is often at its most spectacular at the ocean edge. It is here that the sea attacks the land and changes the landscape. The sea is like a battering ram and the sand particles it carries act like a grindstone as they erode the shore. The waves force air into cracks in the rocks, widening the cracks and eventually breaking up the rock face. New land can also be created at the ocean's edge. The great rivers drop their sediment here – loads of mud, rock and sand. If the amount of sediment is too great to be carried away by the sea, it forms a muddy plain called a delta. Sometimes sediment dumps form at the river's mouth. When this happens, the river is forced to branch out into smaller streams to flow around them. This creates a delta shaped like a bird's foot.

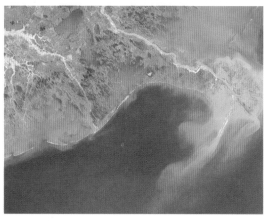

Bird-foot delta
A view from Space showing how the Mississippi River has dropped its sediment to form this huge bird-foot delta. See how plumes of light-coloured sediment have spilled out into the Gulf of Mexico.

A riverboat chugs down the Mississippi River in Louisiana, USA. The river carries vast quantities of mud. You can tell this from the colour of the water. This mud will become part of the Mississippi delta.

Sea caves and arches

A coastal scene in Normandy, France. The soft chalky cliffs are continually being eroded, or worn away, by the relentless attack of the sea. In some places caves have been carved out of the bottom of cliffs, and arches have been sculptured just offshore (*below right*). This is because some parts of the cliffs are made from softer rock than the rest, and these rocks are eroded more quickly by the battering waves. In the same way, bays are created by the sea pounding onto softer rocks. Where rocks are harder, they resist erosion and form headlands jutting out into the sea.

Black sandcastles

Sand is a feature of many seashores. Here on Lanzarote, one of the Canary Islands, the beaches are black. The island is volcanic in origin, which means it formed from molten rock that rose up from the ocean floor. Ordinary sand is formed from tiny grains of light-coloured rock, seashells and coral. The volcanic sand is made up of minute grains of the dark volcanic rock, basalt.

THE CHANGING COASTLINE

You will need: sand, plastic bucket, water tank, water jug.

The great rivers of the world remove millions of tonnes of mud, rock and sand from the land every day and transport them into the sea. If the rivers flow slowly into the sea, they dump this sediment over a broad area shaped like a fan, called a delta. You can copy this natural process when you make your own delta. The flowing water cuts its way deeply through the sand at first. Then, as it starts to lose speed, it divides into lots of channels. As the water slows down, it drops the sand it is carrying as sediment. After a while, this will take on the shape of a fan, or delta. In delta regions, the land is gradually advancing into the sea. Elsewhere, the opposite is happening. The sea is advancing into the land as the waves wear the coastline away. We examine how this happens in the first project. Sea defences are often built to protect the land, but it is very difficult to withstand the power of the waves.

Making waves

1 Mix a little water with the sand in a bucket until it is quite wet and sticks firmly together. Then pack the sand in a wedge shape at one end of the tank.

2 Carefully pour water into the empty end of the tank so as not to disturb the sand too much. Fill the tank until the water level comes about two-thirds up the sloping sand.

3 Make gentle waves in the water on the side opposite the sand. Notice how the waves gradually wear away the sloping sand. This is what happens on a sandy seashore.

Making a delta

1 Trim the cardboard container so that it is about 10–15 cm deep. Now take the bin liners to make the box waterproof.

2 Cover the inside of the box with the bin liners and tape securely at each end. Make sure the seal between the bin liners is secure.

3 Using the trowel, spread sand over the bottom of the tray until it is about 4-5 cm deep. Flatten it with the trowel until it is smooth.

4 Rest one end of the container on a block of wood or something similar to make a slope. Pour water from the jug onto the sand in the middle of the higher end.

M A T E R I A L S

You will need: scissors, long cardboard container, 2 plastic bin liners, sticky tape, trowel, sand, water jug.

If you continue pouring, you will find that the water gradually washes away a path through the sand. It deposits sand it has washed away at the lower end in a delta region.

ISLANDS

Many islands are found scattered around the oceans. Some are known as continental islands. They stand in shallow seas and were once joined to the continents. For example, Greenland was once joined to North America, and the British Isles were once part of mainland Europe. Some islands, called land-tied islands, lie tucked in close to the shore. They are tied to the shore by a sand bar, like a causeway. Other islands lie far away from the continents in the middle of the oceans. These oceanic islands were formed by volcanic action continuing over many years. Some, such as the Hawaiian Islands, grew up over volcanic hot spots in the Earth's crust. Others, such as Iceland, lie in regions where volcanic activity is taking place at plate boundaries.

Many different corals live in this coral garden in the Solomon Islands in the Pacific Ocean. The corals are beautiful, but have hundreds of stinging tentacles to kill their prey.

How a coral atoll develops
Coral grows in the shallow waters around a volcanic island.

The island sinks or the sea rises, but the coral continues to grow.

The island completely disappears. This leaves a ring of coral around a lagoon, which we call a coral atoll.

Coral circle
Circular atolls, or coral islands, are found dotted around the warm Indian and Pacific Oceans. They first grow up around a volcanic island, then they continue growing as the island gradually sinks into the sea.

Tied to the land

The island of Mont St Michel lies close to the coast of Brittany in northwest France. It is a classic example of a land-tied island. Land-tied islands are offshore islands connected to the shore by a sand bar that has been deposited by currents. Mont St Michel is joined to the mainland by a raised road, or causeway, about 1.5 km long.

Hot and cold

This is one of many hot springs found in Iceland. Iceland is a volcanic island located at the point where the Mid-Atlantic Ridge rises to the surface of the sea. Water, heated by the hot rock underground, comes to the surface as hot springs.

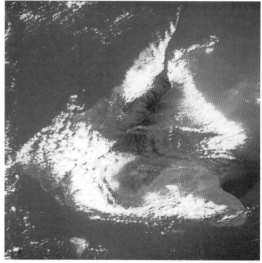

Big smoky

The Big Island of Hawaii. Smoke pours out from erupting volcanoes. The Hawaiian Islands are all tips of underwater volcanoes, which erupted on the ocean floor and rose to the surface.

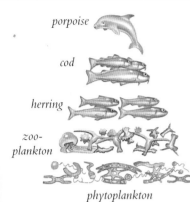

porpoise

cod

herring

zoo-
plankton

phytoplankton

LIFE IN THE OCEANS

Life on Earth began in the oceans about 3,000 million years ago. However, it took a long time before organisms similar to those found today made their first appearance. We find traces of them in rocks about 600 million years old. They include simple animals such as jellyfish and worms. Today, the seas are full of millions of different species of animals. Almost all of them ultimately depend on simple plants, called phytoplankton, for their food. The phytoplankton float in the seawater where tiny animals, called zooplankton, graze on them. Larger animals consume the zooplankton, and are then eaten themselves by larger animals still. Each animal is a link in a chain. This is known as a food chain.

Ocean pyramid
This food pyramid shows the feeding relationships in an ocean food chain. Simple plants, phytoplankton, are eaten in large amounts by zooplankton. Tiny zooplankton are then eaten by the next level in the chain, herrings. Herrings, in turn, are eaten by cod. Finally, porpoises prey on cod.

Animal tree
This illustration shows the main animal groups that live in the seas, from simple single-celled creatures, such as protozoa, to vertebrates, larger back-boned fish and mammals. It is arranged in the shape of a tree, with the different groups shown on different branches.

Moss animals

Molluscs

Vertebrates

Brachiopods

Crustacea

Echinoderms

Roundworms

Segmen
wor

Coelenterates

Flatworms

Sponges

Protozoa

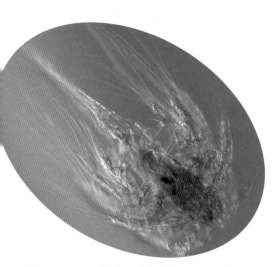

Microscopic zooplankton like this are near the bottom of the ocean food chain. They feed on equally small plant life called phytoplankton, which are tiny floating algae.

Tiny crustaceans
Tiny crustaceans are found in huge numbers in the oceans. Many of these are called krill, the tiny shrimp-like creatures that are the main food for most baleen whales.

Open wide
Humpback whales feeding. You can see the plates of baleen which are used to filter small creatures from the seawater. Humpbacks also eat small fish such as herring. Whales are at the top of the food chain because they have no natural enemies, apart from human beings.

SHORE LIFE

Well-drilled
Dog whelks preying on barnacles. The dog whelk bores through the shell of the barnacle to get at the soft body inside.

FACT BOX
• The seaweed known as the Pacific giant kelp can grow as much as 45 cm in a day and can eventually reach a length of 60 m.

• Molluscs cause erosion by digging little pits in the rocks as they feed on seaweed.

• Seaweed was for many years the main source of the element iodine.

The seashore is a challenging habitat for living things. It is constantly pounded by the waves, exposed to salt spray, and alternately covered then uncovered by the tide. Yet a remarkable number of animals and plants live in this habitat. The kind of species found depends on the type of shore. A feature of rocky shores is seaweed, which attaches itself to rocks. Seaweeds are examples of algae, the simplest types of plant life. Many kinds of crabs and molluscs, such as limpets and whelks, also live on rocky shores. Crabs and a few molluscs, such as clams, are active on sandy shores, too, but the main residents there live under the surface and include many kinds of worms.

Mangroves in the Florida Everglades. Mangroves grow at the ocean edge in tropical regions. As they grow, they send down roots from their branches, eventually forming a tangled thicket. These thickets are home to creatures such as mudskippers, a type of fish.

Mudskippers

A mudskipper travelling over the muddy surface in a mangrove swamp. Mudskippers get their name from their habit of skipping across the mud, using their front fins as legs and flicking their tails. These remarkable creatures are fish that not only walk but can also breathe air out of water.

A female sea lion lounges on a beach. This beautiful and intelligent mammal moves about slowly and clumsily on land, but in the sea it swims swiftly and gracefully because of its streamlined body.

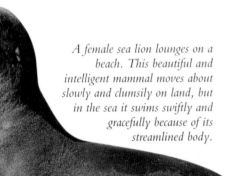

Scurrying scavengers

Crabs scavenging for food on the shore of the Galápagos Islands. Crabs are crustaceans, with their soft bodies protected by hard shells. They have five pairs of jointed legs. The front pair of legs has strong pincer-like claws, which they use to grasp prey. There are over 4,500 species of crabs found throughout the world.

ON THE SHORE

For the nature detective, the seashore is a fascinating place. Whether the shore is sandy, muddy, pebbly or rocky, it usually teems with life. Creatures may be found scurrying on the surface, hiding under rocks in rock pools or burrowing in the sand. The shore will also reveal many traces of previous life. For example, on most shores you will find crab claws, cuttlefish bones and all kinds of shells, such as those of clams, mussels, limpets, barnacles and many snail-like creatures. Each of these creatures has a different kind of shell, which is grown to protect their soft bodies. Many shells look lovely on the inside, as well as the outside, as you will discover for yourself in one of these projects. You will also find out that shells are made of calcium carbonate. Shellfish take this chemical from the sea as they grow.

You will need: gloves, plastic bucket, fishing net, spade, plastic bags, magnifying glass, notebook and pencil, field guides, binoculars.

Searching for life

1 On most seashores you will find plenty of shells. See how many different kinds of shell you can find and identify. Make sure they are empty before removing them.

2 On the rocks, you will also find many kinds of living shells. The one in the middle of the picture is a limpet, which sticks very strongly to rocks to avoid being swept out to sea.

3 You can often find creatures hiding under loose rocks in rock pools. Always replace the rocks to avoid causing damage to the habitat and to the animals underneath.

4 Crabs are among the most common animals found in rock pools. It is best to hold them across the back of the shell. Then they will not be able to nip you.

5 Many kinds of worms live in the shore sands. They burrow deep when the tide goes out, leaving holes. Dig down where you see holes to find out which worms made them.

6 When you return from the seaside, you will have more time to look at the objects you collected. Use field guides to help you identify the shells, seaweed and skeletons.

Shells with a spiral structure inside.

What is inside a shell?
You can see how different shells are made up by rubbing them against coarse sandpaper or a flat metal file. Gradually wear away the outside layers to reveal the structure inside. Try and find shells with a beautiful spiral structure inside.

The acid test
To find out what shells are made of, scrape a shell with a file and collect the powder in a plastic lid. Add vinegar to the powder. It will start to fizz. This tells you it is made of calcium carbonate because acids attack alkaline carbonates, producing a gas, carbon dioxide.

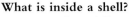

SEA BIRDS

The sea cliffs and shore provide a storehouse of food for bird life. There are shoals of fish in the surface waters, while on the shore and nearby marshes and mudflats, there are burrowing worms, molluscs and crustaceans. Seabirds, such as albatrosses and shearwaters, spend most of their life out at sea, returning to land only to breed. Gulls, cormorants and puffins remain in coastal waters and are often seen on or near the shore. The other main shore birds are waders, which probe about for food at the water's edge. These birds include avocets, oystercatchers and sandpipers. In winter, these habitats are visited by vast flocks of migrants escaping from the cold elsewhere. Huge numbers of greylag and barnacle geese spend the winter on the estuary mudflats and saltwater marshes around the coasts of Britain.

A black-browed albatross in the Falkland Islands off southern South America. Albatrosses are big seabirds with a large wingspan. They are able to glide effortlessly for long periods over great distances.

Crowd trouble
Atlantic gannets crowd together at their nest site, squabbling frequently. There is often a shortage of nest sites on the shore.

FACT BOX

• The Arctic tern holds the world record for long-distance travel. It migrates some 35,000 km each year between the Arctic and Antarctic.

• Gannets fish by diving into the water from heights of up to 30 m.

• Cormorants may dive as deep as 50 m when hunting for fish.

• The wandering albatross has the biggest wingspan of any bird, measuring 3.5 m.

• The male Emperor penguin incubates the single egg laid by its mate by tucking it under a flap of skin on its belly.

Here a puffin enjoys its latest catch of fish. Puffins have large bills, which become highly coloured in the breeding season. The female lays her eggs in burrows dug in cliff tops.

Sifting mud

The avocet is one of the larger and more beautiful of the waders. It has long legs for wading and a long bill curved at the end for sifting in the mud for small aquatic animals. Its upturned bill and striking black and white plumage make it easy to recognize.

Gentoo penguins diving into the sea in Antarctica. Penguins have a streamlined body for swimming in the water, where they have been known to reach speeds of up to 40 km per hour. They use their flipper-shaped wings as paddles in the water.

WATCHING THE BIRDS

You will need: long and short bamboo canes, ball of twine, large sand-coloured sheet, safety pins, scissors, binoculars.

At the seaside you will see two main groups of birds – true seabirds such as gulls, and waders such as sanderlings. Seabirds have short legs and webbed feet, which they use for swimming. You can often spot seabirds out at sea, diving for food. In general, they have strong sharp bills, or beaks, for grasping and tearing at the fish they catch. Waders are quite different. Their feet are not webbed and they usually have long legs for wading in the water. You will see them near the water's edge, particularly on the marshes and the mudflats at the mouth of a river. They use their long bills to probe the sand and mud for food.

One of the main methods of identifying birds is by their plumage, or covering of feathers. But looking at the legs, feet and bills of birds will tell you a lot about them, too. Try and get as close to the birds as you can when you go out birdwatching. If you make a hide for observation and keep very quiet, the birds will take no notice of you.

Making a hide

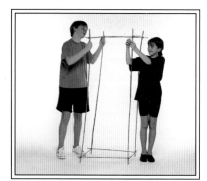

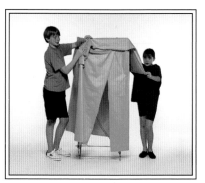

1 Find a place above the high tide level. Push four long canes firmly into the sand to make a square. Using twine, tie four short canes between the uprights top and bottom.

2 To help make the frame stronger, tie some more long canes diagonally on each side, for example, from the bottom left corner to the top right corner.

3 Now carefully drape the large sheet over the bamboo frame. Secure the sheet firmly at the corners, both top and bottom, with twine. The hide is almost complete.

Tracking birds

See if you can identify the birds that have left tracks in the mud or sand. On the shore, lay a sheet of acetate over the tracks and trace them. At home, copy the tracks into a notebook. Use a field guide to identify them.

The sanderling is one of the most common shore birds. Unlike most other small waders, it does not have a rear toe, just three toes pointing forwards. This means its tracks look quite different from those of other waders.

4 Carefully pin the ends of the sheet together with the safety pins. Remember to leave one or more holes for you and your friends to look through.

5 You will be able to identify birds that come close to the hide just with your eyes. However, binoculars are handy for looking at birds farther away.

LIFE IN THE OPEN SEA

A marlin leaps high out of the water. The long 'spear' on its mouth can be clearly seen. It is thought the spear is used to maim its prey.

In the surface waters of most oceans, it is light and the water is relatively warm. As you go deeper, it gets darker and colder, and the pressure increases rapidly. It is in the upper 200 m of these oceans, in the sunlight zone, that marine life flourishes. This is where plankton thrive and support the ocean food chains. Jellyfish, prawns, and fish such as herring and tuna can all be found here. These fish are eaten by predators such as barracudas and sharks. Further down, in the dimly lit twilight zone, there are squid and octopus. No light at all can reach depths below 1,000 m, yet life still exists. Strange-looking fish with fierce inward-curving teeth, such as viperfish and hatchet fish, survive. There are also angler fish with luminous 'light bulbs' to lure their prey. Finally, worms and shrimp-like creatures feed on the seabed.

FACT BOX

• Some squid escape their enemies by squirting a browny-black ink at them.

• The giant squid is the world's largest invertebrate, or animal without a backbone. It can reach over 12 m in length.

• The ocean sunfish produces up to 30 million eggs when it spawns. Each egg measures just over 1 mm in diameter.

• The world's largest fish is the whale shark. It can grow to over 12 m in length and can weigh up to 15 tonnes.

• The sailfish can swim at speeds of 70 km per hour and is thought to be the fastest fish.

Using their very large fins as wings, flying fish can glide through the air above the waves for distances of 30 m or more. The fish launches itself into the air with a flick of its strong tail. Flying fish live in the warm tropical regions around the world.

A deep-sea angler fish, showing the light above its head and its huge mouth and teeth. This angler fish has changed colour since it was caught. In real life, it is as pitch black as the sea that surrounds it. Its light is produced by light-producing organs, called esca. In some species, the light can be much longer than the fish's body. The light attracts other fish, which are gobbled up by the angler fish. Although they look so fierce, most of these deep-sea angler fish are small. Small enough, in fact, to fit into the palm of your hand.

The octopus is so-called because it has eight tentacles. On each it has one or two rows of sucker discs, which it uses to handle its prey when hunting and feeding. The tentacles are also used for moving about on the seabed. The octopus swims by water-jet propulsion. It squirts out water from an opening in its head called a siphon.

The razor-sharp teeth of the great white shark are deadly. They can cut through flesh with ease. Most sharks have several rows of teeth, which are shed and replaced row by row. The great white shark is famous for being extremely dangerous to humans. However, it usually feeds on fish, turtles and seals.

SEA MAMMALS

Bottle-nosed dolphins adapt well to human companionship and can be easily trained.

The most advanced of the animal groups on Earth are the mammals. They are warm-blooded and breathe air. Females give birth to live young. They suckle their young, feeding them with milk. Mammals mainly live on land, but there are a number that thrive in the sea, including whales, the largest mammals of all. Dolphins, porpoises, seals and sea lions are sea mammals, too. They are all well adapted to their watery habitat. Sea mammals have an insulating layer of fatty tissue, called blubber, under their skin to keep out the cold. All the sea mammals swim fast and gracefully. The killer whale (which is actually a dolphin) can reach speeds of up to 50 km an hour. Seals and sea lions slide and wriggle when they come on land. They find climbing difficult, but they can move nimbly over a rocky shore.

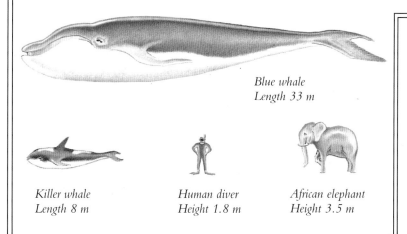

Blue whale
Length 33 m

Killer whale
Length 8 m

Human diver
Height 1.8 m

African elephant
Height 3.5 m

The blue whale is the largest animal ever to live. It can grow to a length of over 33 m and can weigh up to 150 tonnes. This is bigger than the largest dinosaur and as long as six or more elephants. The blue whale can only reach this incredible size because its body is supported by the water. Without this support, the weight of the blue whale's body would crush its internal organs.

FACT BOX

• Humpback whales blow bubbles as they swim in a spiral under a school of fish. This frightens the fish and they start swimming really close together. Then the humpback surfaces in the middle of the fish with its mouth wide open, and swallows them up.

• The sperm whale can dive to depths of 3,000 m to find food. It can remain underwater for two hours before coming up to the surface to breathe.

• The humpback whale communicates over distances of more than 100 km by singing its own unique song. The song can last up to 30 minutes.

A humpback whale breaching, or leaping, out of the water. To do so, it accelerates through the water and then flicks its tail, which takes it up to, and above, the surface. For an animal weighing tens of tonnes, this is a remarkable feat. No one knows why whales breach. It is probably a way of communicating, as the loud splash can be heard many kilometres away.

A killer whale surges up to the shore hunting elephant seals. The killer whale is one of the few whales that come right up to the shore on purpose. In some regions, such as the Crozet Islands in the Indian Ocean, they swim up onto the beach to grab baby sea lions.

A monk seal swims gracefully in Hawaiian waters, using its flippers as paddles. Its body is well streamlined, so it can slip through the water easily.

LIFE ON A CORAL REEF

This coral is found in the Red Sea, which lies between Africa and Arabia. The Red Sea is famed for its colourful coral reefs, which thrive in the warm waters of the region.

Coral reefs are found in tropical and sub-tropical regions of the world. The tiny animals that build them can only exist if the water is more than 18°C. Coral is built by tiny jelly-like animals, called polyps. When they grow, they extract calcium from the sea and deposit it as hard, limey cups around their bodies. When they die, other polyps grow on the limey remains, and slowly a reef builds up. Coral reefs are one of the oceans' richest habitats. They provide plentiful food and shelter and are home to a host of different species, such as sea anemones, sponges, starfish and giant clams, which grow up to a metre wide. Colourful fish are in abundance, and vicious moray eels prowl for food. Other animals, including parrot fish, eat the coral and severely damage the reef.

FACT BOX

• The Great Barrier Reef in Australia measures some 2,000 km long and covers an area of over 200,000 sq km.

• The crown-of-thorns starfish eats coral and can devastate reefs. The Great Barrier Reef is now badly affected by this creature.

• Most coral reefs are found in warm waters between the Tropic of Cancer in the Northern Hemisphere and the Tropic of Capricorn in the Southern Hemisphere.

• Starfish are not fish, but creatures called echinoderms, which means they have spiny skins. Most starfish have five arms and hundreds, or even thousands, of tube feet.

Safety in numbers
A shoal of fish, called antheas, stick close to their coral reef home. These small fish would be easy targets for larger predators if they were on their own, but together they confuse their attackers. This is why many species of fish move in shoals.

The head of a moray eel, one of the top predators in coral reefs. It has a large mouth and powerful teeth for catching prey. Some species can grow up to 3 m long.

A giant clam on a coral reef at Heron Island, Australia. Its hinged shell can weigh as much as a quarter of a tonne.

A clown fish nestles among the stinging tentacles of a sea anemone. No predators dare come near for fear of being stung. The clown fish is quite safe and the anemone benefits by picking up food scraps dropped by the fish. This two-way partnership between two different species is called symbiosis.

SHIPS

Ships have been sailing the oceans for at least 5,000 years. Today, they are still the main method of transporting goods and materials between countries overseas. Merchant ships carry goods, while naval ships are designed for fighting. Once built of wood and powered by sails, most ships are now built from steel plates welded together and powered by diesel engines or steam turbines. Cruise ships do not look like merchant ships. Cabins, shops and restaurants are built up high above main deck level. This part of a ship is called the superstructure. Bulk carriers, such as oil tankers, have little superstructure. Their cargo is carried in large tanks, or holds, below deck.

Tall ships
Ships gather in a harbour in Sweden to celebrate the golden age of sail (mid-1800s). The two large, square riggers are used as training ships for ocean sailors.

A flotilla, or small fleet, of tugs towing an oil rig along a river in Louisiana, USA, towards the sea. Tugs are small, tough and powerful vessels that are easy to handle in difficult conditions.

FACT BOX

• The longest passenger liner ever built is the *Norway*. It measures 315.5 m in length and was built in 1960.

• Clippers were the swiftest sailing ships. They were built in the 1800s to carry goods between the Far East and the Americas.

• The fastest crossing of the Atlantic was made by the power boat *Destriero* in 1992. It took 2 days, 10 hours and 35 minutes.

Twin hulls

A catamaran ferry, which carries passengers quickly and comfortably. A catamaran can travel fast because it has two slim hulls, instead of the single broad hull of a normal boat. With less hull in the water, it suffers from less drag and can therefore travel faster.

Handy containers

A container ship with its deck piled high with containers. Although they can be filled with a variety of cargo, containers are always the same size so they can be easily loaded onto trucks and trains.

Skimming the waves

A hydrofoil passenger ferry travelling at speed. Hydrofoils have underwater wings called foils, which lift the hull, or main body of the ship, out of the water. The faster the speed of the ship, the greater the lift as it skims over the water.

FLOATING AND HOVERING

MATERIALS

You will need: scissors, coloured paper, drinking straw, sticky tape, modelling clay, water tank.

Until early in the last century, ships were built of wood. This seems sensible because wood is lighter than water and floats on top of it. Most ships today, however, are built of steel, which is much heavier than water. Some ships, such as aircraft carriers and tankers, weigh hundreds of thousands of tonnes. So how can they float? They float because of upthrust, a force in the water that holds things up. Anything will float if the upthrust on it is greater than its own weight. This is the basic principle behind ship design. The first project shows you that giving a ship a broad hull increases the upthrust on it and allows it to float. Some sea vessels do not float, they hover. They glide on a cushion of air above the water and can travel very fast.

Which will float – a solid ball or a hollowed out bowl of modelling clay?

Shaping a ship

1 Make a sail by cutting a triangle out of the coloured paper and taping the straw to the middle of it. Roll the modelling clay into a ball and stick your sail in it.

2 Fill the tank with water and put your sailing ship in it. You will find it sinks like a stone immediately. Building a ship out of a solid heavy material does not work!

3 Try again, but hollow out the modelling clay into a bowl shape. Stick in the sail and place it in the tank. This time it will float.

MATERIALS

You will need: brick, plastic bag, spring balance, notebook and pencil, water tank.

Hovering

Turn a cold glass upside-down on a wet tray and push it with a finger. It will not move much. Now dip it in hot water from the tap and try again. The glass will slide around easily.

This is because hot air is escaping around the bottom, and the glass is hovering like a hovercraft.

Measuring upthrust

1 Place the brick in the plastic bag and hang it from the spring balance. Make a note of how heavy the brick is by watching where the pointer comes to on the scale.

2 Repeat the experiment, but this time lower the brick into the water tank until it is submerged. This time you will find the reading will be lower than before because of the upthrust of the water on the brick.

A hovercraft ferry heads across the English Channel. It is gliding along on a cushion of air.

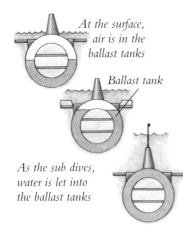

At the surface, air is in the ballast tanks

Ballast tank

As the sub dives, water is let into the ballast tanks

When the submarine is submerged, the ballast tanks are full

Ballast tanks
Submarines dive by filling their ballast tanks with water. They surface by releasing water from their ballast tanks and replacing it with air.

SUBMARINES

Submarines are able to travel silently beneath the surface of the water. Most of them are naval vessels. They are ideal for warfare because they are designed to creep up on their targets without being seen. Submarines have an enclosed hull, which is smooth and streamlined to allow them to slip through the water easily. They have a small raised superstructure called the conning tower, which houses the bridge used for navigation and other operations. A periscope is used to look above the surface when the submarine is shallowly submerged. A submarine dives and surfaces by letting water in, or pumping water out of ballast tanks. Smaller civilian submarines, called submersibles, are used for deep-sea research work and to assist diving operations, by transporting divers down to the seabed.

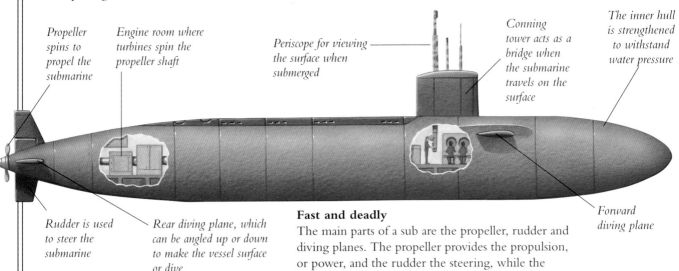

Propeller spins to propel the submarine

Engine room where turbines spin the propeller shaft

Periscope for viewing the surface when submerged

Conning tower acts as a bridge when the submarine travels on the surface

The inner hull is strengthened to withstand water pressure

Rudder is used to steer the submarine

Rear diving plane, which can be angled up or down to make the vessel surface or dive

Forward diving plane

Fast and deadly
The main parts of a sub are the propeller, rudder and diving planes. The propeller provides the propulsion, or power, and the rudder the steering, while the diving planes are used in diving and surfacing.

Nuclear powered

This is one of the large nuclear submarines of the US Navy. It is powered by a nuclear reactor, which heats water into steam in a boiler. The steam then drives a turbine that spins the propeller. Nuclear submarines can stay submerged for months at a time without surfacing.

Diving submersible

Mini-subs called submersibles are used in scientific research and in underwater salvage and construction work. Usually, they have a crew of two or three and dive for a day or less.

Deepest diver

The bathyscaphe, deep-diving vessel, *Trieste* made the deepest ocean descent ever in 1960. It dived into the Mariana Trench in the Pacific Ocean, reaching a depth of 10,916 m.

UP PERISCOPE

M A T E R I A L S

Submarines are deadly warships because they can travel beneath the surface of the water to approach their target without being spotted. Submarine commanders need to know what is happening on the surface, however, so submarines are fitted with a periscope. This gives the commander an all-round view of the surface while the submarine stays hidden underwater, waiting for the moment to attack. A periscope uses two mirrors to reflect light down a long tube into the commander's eye, and a telescope to magnify distant objects. It can move up and down as well as in a complete circle. Observations are made when the submarine is underwater, with just the tip of the periscope peeping out above the waves. You can make your own periscope to help you to look round corners and over walls without being seen.

You will need: ruler, pencil, large piece of stiff card, scissors, sticky tape, two flat mirrors.

Make a periscope

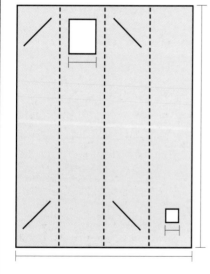

Follow the dimensions shown in this plan to make your periscope.

1 Mark the card into four equal segments, as shown on the plan *(left)*. Carefully score along the marks using the back of the scissors. This will help when folding.

2 In the two segments shown on the plan, cut out slots for the mirrors at a 45° angle. Ask an adult to cut out the eyehole and viewing window in the other two segments.

Zig-zag light

This diagram shows the path of a beam of light through a periscope. Light enters the periscope through the window at the top and is reflected downwards by the top mirror onto the bottom mirror. This mirror in turn reflects the light through the eyehole into the viewer's eye.

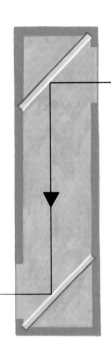

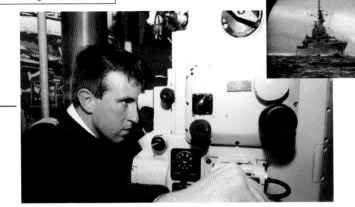

Periscope view

At periscope depth, a submarine officer can check what is happening on the surface through the periscope. The black and white picture *(top right)* is what the officer can actually see.

5 Now your periscope is ready for action. You can use it to look over high walls and hedges and peek round corners.

3 Fold the card along the score marks to make it into a square tube. Tape up the edges firmly, both inside and out. Cut out square cards and tape these to the top and bottom.

4 Carefully push the mirrors into the slots at the top and bottom of the tube. Securely tape them to keep them firm. Make sure they face out of the eyehole and viewing window!

DIVING

The sea is not a natural habitat for humans, used to breathing air and surrounded by a light, warm atmosphere. It is cold and, as you go deeper, the pressure on your body gets greater and greater due to the weight of water. Today, using modern diving equipment, scuba divers can dive to a depth of 50 m. This is not particularly deep, but it is the safe limit for air-breathing scuba divers. Scuba stands for self-contained underwater breathing apparatus. To protect themselves from the cold, scuba divers usually wear all-enclosing suits. Depending on the length or depth of the dive, a diver might wear an electrically heated suit. If scuba divers breathe a special mix of gases, depths of 600 m are possible. One thousand metres has been achieved by divers using special experimental chambers.

Scuba diving
A scuba diver explores a wreck on the seabed. Divers wear a face mask and breathe through a pipe carrying air under pressure, stored in tanks worn on the back.

Shallow breathing
Children snorkelling. A snorkel is held over the mouth. It has an air pipe, which allows the face to be submerged underwater while still breathing air through the pipe

A pearl nestling in its shell. Pearls form inside the shells of pearl oysters, shellfish that live in tropical seas. They form when the oyster makes a coating around irritating particles that enter its shell.

Pearl diving

This diver has been diving for pearl oysters on the seabed off the coast of Australia. He is wearing a heavy diving suit so he can walk on the bottom. He is supplied with air through a hose from an air pump on board the boat. It is his vital life-support system.

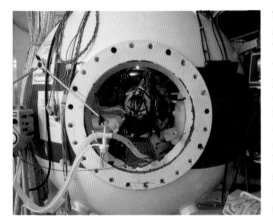

Under compression

When divers work for long periods at great depths, they rest in an underwater compression chamber like this because it takes so long to adjust to the lower surface pressure.

FACT BOX

• For every 10 m a diver descends into the sea, the pressure increases by 1 atmosphere (the pressure at the surface).

• When the bathyscaphe *Trieste* dived to a depth of nearly 11,000 m in the Pacific Ocean in 1960, it had to withstand a water pressure of more than 1 tonne on every square centimetre of its hull.

• For deep dives, divers breathe a mixture of helium and oxygen to prevent nitrogen narcosis, a dangerous condition caused by excess nitrogen in the blood. Breathing this mixture gives divers squeaky voices that sound just like Donald Duck's.

DIVE, DIVE, DIVE

People began diving and working on the seabed long before there were proper diving suits. The earliest diving device they used was called a diving bell. Diving bells for deep diving are fed with air under pressure to keep water out. Pressure is an important feature in two of the items featured here. When operating your diver, squeezing the sides of the jar forces water into the little tube, compressing the air inside. With more water in it, the tube becomes less buoyant and sinks. If real divers have been breathing air under pressure for some time and then surface too quickly, they suffer from the bends. When the pressure is released, gas in their blood bubbles out, causing muscle pain, paralysis, coma, or even death.

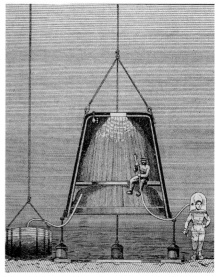

This print shows a diving bell designed by the scientist Sir Edmund Halley in 1690. Air was piped from it into the diver's helmet.

The diving bell

Turn a glass upside-down and push it downwards into a tank of water. The trapped air inside stops most of the water getting in. The diving bell works in a similar way, with more air being pumped in as the diver uses it up.

The bends

Pointing a fizzy drinks bottle away from your face, slowly unscrew the cap. You will see bubbles of gas appear. The gas was dissolved under pressure in the drink. When the pressure was released it bubbled out. If divers rise to the surface too quickly, nitrogen in their blood bubbles out in a similar way. This is what causes the bends.

Make a diver

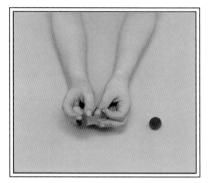

1 Stick modelling clay around the mouth of the small tube on the outside, to weigh it down. You may need to add or take away some clay later as a result of your test in step 2.

2 Transfer the tube to the test jar. Let water into it, but leave a bubble of air at the top so that when you let it go, it just floats. You may need to add or take away some clay.

3 When you have made sure the tube is floating correctly, put your thumb over the mouth of it under water and carefully lift it out of the water.

4 Transfer the tube to the sweet jar, which should be filled with water to the very top. Place the tube in the water and take your thumb away. Now screw on the lid.

MATERIALS

You will need: modelling clay, small tube, large open jar for testing, plastic sweet jar with lid.

5 Squeeze the sides of the jar tightly. The tube will dive to the bottom because the pressure forces water into the tube, making it less buoyant. Take your hands away and the tube will rise again.

THE SEA'S RESOURCES

Fishermen haul in a net bulging with fish. An estimated 80 million tonnes of fish are caught in the world's oceans each year. However, overfishing has led to shortages.

The sea is vast and has abundant resources that we can use. The most obvious one is fish. Fish have always been part of the human diet. They are rich in protein, oils, vitamins and minerals. The sea is a great storehouse of chemicals, including sodium, chlorine, magnesium and bromine. Salt can be extracted by evaporating the water in shallow salt pans. There are also many precious resources that lie hidden under the seabed, such as oil and natural gas. These fossil fuels lie trapped in the rocks and are extracted by drilling. The seas are a potentially major source of energy. Already tidal power is used with some success and there are plans for using the heat from warm waters to drive turbines.

People working in a salt pan in Thailand. In salt panning, seawater is let into shallow basins or ponds along the coast. The heat of the Sun gradually evaporates the seawater and the salt is left behind.

Desalination plants provide drinking water in hot desert countries in the Middle East, where water shortages occur. Desalination, which means taking salt out, involves heating seawater so that it boils. The steam produced is then cooled to give pure liquid water.

Fossil fuels

A North Sea gas rig. Most gas and oil wells lie on the continental shelves in relatively shallow waters, such as the North Sea, the Gulf of Mexico, the Caribbean and the Gulf of Guinea.

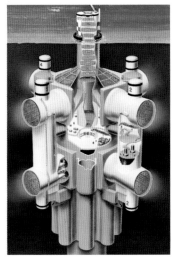

OTEC

A design for a floating energy plant called OTEC (ocean thermal energy conversion). The principle behind this massive plant is to use the heat energy in surface waters. The hot water is used to evaporate a liquid into gas. The resulting gas would drive turbines that could produce electricity.

Tidal power

This is La Rance Tidal Power Station near St Malo in France, the first tidal power station to be built. Tidal power uses the continual ebbing and flowing of the tides as a power source to drive electricity generators.

SAVING THE SEAS

A satellite view of the Netherlands, a very low-lying country. Due to air pollution the Earth is getting warmer, which may cause sea levels to rise. As a result, the Netherlands could be completely flooded.

People once thought the oceans were so vast that whatever they did to them it would make no difference. They dumped their rubbish into the sea and expanded their fishing fleets to catch more fish and whales for food. Unfortunately, it has all begun to go wrong. Fish catches have dropped and some whale species have come close to extinction. Serious accidents have occurred with oil tankers polluting beaches and killing marine life.

Environmental groups throughout the world have started to make their voices heard to try to resolve some of these problems. There are now signs that governments all over the world are becoming more aware of these issues. Most countries have banned or restricted the killing of whales and have introduced fishing quotas, or restrictions, to reduce the world's fish catches. Some marine habitats are now being protected, and techniques have been pioneered to cope with oil spills and pollution. These are only the first steps. Much more still needs to be done to protect the future of the oceans.

Workers trying to cope with the effects of an oil tanker disaster in Alaska. The oil gets stickier the longer it is left, making it more difficult to shift and reducing the chances of survival for affected wildlife.

FACT BOX

• In the 1970s, tuna fishermen used to catch hundreds of thousands of dolphins in their nets every year. Now, most use nets with a specially designed fine-mesh panel that the dolphins leap over to escape.

• Many marine species, from corals and giant clams to marine turtles and whales, are now protected by international organizations such as CITES, the Convention on International Trade in Endangered Species.

Great coral
Tourist planes anchored off the Great Barrier Reef in northeast Australia. Extending for some 2,000 km, this is the largest coral reef in the world. Although the Reef has international protection as a world heritage site, increased tourism has put it under threat. The coral grows in shallow waters and can be easily damaged by tourist ships, amateur divers and drilling for oil.

Fish farming in a Scottish sea loch. Fish farming like this does not conserve fish stocks in the open sea. However, farmed fish do supplement the amount of fish that is available. Salmon, trout and oysters are not as rare as they used to be.

Tourists follow a school of whales as they feed in Alaskan waters. Tours like this increase awareness of the whaling problem. Whales are still needlessly slaughtered by some countries, threatening the extinction of many species.

INDEX

albatrosses 38
algae 34
Andes 12
angler fish 42-3
animals 32-7
Antarctic Ocean 8-9
arches, rock 4, 27
Arctic Ocean 8-9
Arctic tern 38
Atlantic Ocean 5, 8-9, 10, 12, 13, 14-15, 31, 48
atolls 30
avocets 38-9

baleen whales 33
ballast 52
barnacle goose 38
barnacles 7, 34
barracudas 42
basalt 27
bathyscapes 53, 57
beach 6
bends 58
bird foot delta 26
birds 38-41
blubber 44
blue whale 44
British Isles 30

calcium 16, 36-7
Caribbean 61
catamarans 49
causeways 30-31
caves 4, 27
Challenger Deep 14-15
chlorine 16, 60
clams 34, 36, 47, 62
cliffs 4, 20, 26-7, 38
clouds 17
cod 32
coelenterates 32
condensation 17
continental drift 10-13

continental islands 30
continental shelf 14
coral 27, 62-3
  atolls 30
  islands 8, 30
  reefs 5, 8, 46-7
crabs 34-5, 36-7
crustaceans 32-3, 35, 38
currents 20-23

Dead Sea 16
deeps, ocean 13-15
deltas 26-9
diving 53, 56-9
diving bells 58-9
dolphins 44, 62
driftwood 6

earthquakes 12, 13, 20
Earth's surface 4, 8, 10-11, 14-15
echinoderms 32, 46
eels 47
endangered species 62-3
energy sources 60-61
environmental
  protection 62-3
Equator 8, 21
erosion 4, 26-7
evaporation 16
Everglades mangrove 34

fish 5, 6, 32-3, 42-3, 46-7, 60, 62
  freshwater 17
  oxygen supply 17
fishing 62-3
flies, seaweed 6
floating 16, 18-19
floods 25, 27
flotillas 48
flying fish 42
food chain 32-3, 42
fossil fuels 60-61
fractures 14-15
freshwater 17, 19

Galápagos Islands 35
gannets 38
gas, natural 60-61
  global warming 62
  gravity 24-5
  Great Barrier
    Reef 46, 63
  Greenland 30
grouper 5
Gulf of Guinea 61
Gulf of Mexico 26, 61

Gulf Stream 20
gulls 38, 40
gypsum 16

hatchet fish 42
Hawaiian Islands 30-31
Heron Island 47
herring 32, 42
hide, making 40-41
high tide 25
high water mark 6
hot rocks 14, 31
hot spots 30-31
hot springs 31
hovercraft 51
humpback whale 5, 33, 44-5
hydrofoils 49
hydrometer 18-19

Iceland 30, 31
Indian Ocean 8-9, 30
islands 30-31

jellyfish 42

kelp 7, 34
killer whale 44-5
krill 33

lagoons 30
land-tied islands 30-31
Lanzarote 27
limpets 34, 36
low tide 25

magnesium 16, 60
mammals 5, 32, 35, 44-5
manganese nodules 14
mangroves 34
marlin 42
marshes 38, 40
Mid-Atlantic Ridge 13, 14-15, 31
mineral resources 14, 16, 60-61
Mississippi River 26
molluscs 32, 34, 38
Moon 24
moray eel 47
mountains 12, 14-15
mudflats 38, 40
mudskipper 34-5
mussels 36

Netherlands 62
Nile, River 27
Normandy 27

North Sea 8, 61
seas 8
ocean thermal energy
  conversion (OTEC)
  60-61
oceans 8-9
octopus 42-3
oil 60-61, 62
oxygen 17
oysters 63

Pacific Ocean 8-9, 12, 14-15, 21, 30, 53
pearl diving 57
penguins 38-9
periscopes 54-5
phytoplankton 32
plains, ocean 14-15
plankton 32-3, 42
plants 6, 33-4
plates, Earth's 10-13, 15, 30
pollution 62-3
polyps 8, 46
porpoises 42, 44
potassium 16
prawns 42
pressure 57-9
protozoa 32
puffins 38-9

raindrop ripples 22
rainfall 17
Red Sea 11, 46
reefs 5, 8, 46-7
resources 14, 16, 60-61
ridges, ocean 13-15
rivers 8, 11, 17, 26-9
rock pools 6
rocks 4, 36

sailfish 42
salmon 63
salt lakes 16
salt water 4, 6, 16, 18-19, 60
  desalination 60
  floating and salt
    density 16, 18-19
sand 26-7
sand bars 30
sanderling 40-41
sandhopper 6
sandpiper 38
satellite observation 14, 20
scuba diving 56
sea anemones 47
sea lions 35, 44-5

seals 44-5
seas 8
seaside 4, 6-7
seaweed 6, 7, 34
sedimentation 26-9
Seven Seas 8
sharks 42-3
shearwaters 38
shells 27, 36-7
ships 5, 48-53
  Plimsoll lines 19
shore 6-7, 26-9, 36-7
smokers 14
snorkelling 56
sodium 16, 60
sodium chloride 16
Solomon Islands 30
sperm whale 44
sponges 32
spring tides 24
squid 42
stacks 4
starfish 46
steamships 5
subduction 13
submarines 52-5
sulphate 16
Sun 24
symbiosis 47

Thames tidal barrier 25
tidal power 60-61
tidal waves 20
tides 6, 7, 24-5
trenches, ocean 13-15
Tropics of Cancer and
  Capricorn 46
trout 63
tugs 48
tuna 42, 62
turtles 62

underwater viewer 7
upthrust 50-51

valleys, ocean 13-15
vents 14
vertebrates 32
viperfish 42
volcanic islands 30-31
volcanoes 13, 14

waders 38-41
water cycle 16-17
waves 6, 20-23
whales 5, 33, 44-5, 62-3
whelks 34
wind 20, 22-3

worms 32, 34, 37, 38, 42

zooplankton 32-3

PICTURE CREDITS
b=bottom, t=top, c=centre, l=left, r=right.
Bruce Coleman
Limited: pages 16bl, 33br, 41tc, 45bl.
Crown Copyright/
MOD: page 55tr.
Environmental Images:
page 60bl. E. T.
Archives: page 5br.
Robin Kerrod: pages
26br, 53bl, 60tl, 61tr.
Mary Evans Picture
Library: page 58tr.
National Maritime
Museum of Grenwich:
page 19br. Nature
Photographers Limited:
pages 26tl, 33tr, 34tl, 35tl, 45tl. Papilio
Photographic: pages 4br, 30tr, 33tl, 35bl, 38tr, 39bl, 39tr, 39br, 46br, 60bl. Quadrant Picture
Library: pages 51br, 61tl. Scipix: page 25bl.
Spacecharts: pages 11br, 14tr, 14bl, 20br, 24tl, 26bl, 31br, 53br, 62tl.
Tom Teegan: page 57bl.
Trip/R. Cracknell:
page 16tr; Trip/
J. Dennis: page 21tr;
Trip/R. Drury: page
20bl; Trip/B Gadsby:
page 35cr; Trip/
H. Rogers: page 31bl;
Trip/D. Saunders: page
47tl; Trip/Trip: page
60br; Trip/J. Wender:
page 56bl. Warren
Photographic/Kim
Taylor: page 22bl. Zefa:
pages 4tr, 5tl, 5tr, 8tl, 8br, 17br, 20tr, 25tl, 25cr, 27cl, 27br, 31tr, 38bl, 42tl, 42br, 43tc, 43tr, 43bl, 44tl, 45br, 46tl, 47tr, 47br, 48bl, 48tr, 49tr, 49cl, 49br, 53tl, 56tl, 57tl, 57tr, 62tr, 63tl, 64bl, 64br.

64